RiverStream

BE SAFE AROUND WATER

BRIDGET HEOS   ILLUSTRATED BY SILVIA BARONCELLI

RiverStream Illustrated
Great Reading • Real Learning

Amicus Illustrated hardcover edition is published by Amicus
P.O. Box 1329, Mankato, MN 56002
www.amicuspublishing.us

RiverStream Publishing reprinted with permission of Amicus Publishing.

Library of Congress Cataloging-in-Publication Data
Heos, Bridget.
 Be safe around water / by Bridget Heos ; illustrated by Silvia Baroncelli.
   pages cm. — (Be safe!)
 Includes bibliographical references.
 Summary: "A young child teaches her toys, dolls, and action figures the water safety rules she has learned"— Provided by publisher.
 ISBN 978-1-60753-448-8 (library binding) —
ISBN 978-1-60753-663-5 (ebook)
 1. Swimming—Safety measures—Juvenile literature.
 I. Baroncelli, Silvia, illustrator. II. Title.
 GV838.53.S24H46 2015
 797.200289—dc23   2013032335

Editor: Rebecca Glaser
Designer: Kathleen Petelinsek

1 2 3 4 5 CG 18 17 16 15 14
RiverStream Publishing–Corporate Graphics,
Mankato, MN—042014
ISBN 978-1-62243-256-1 (paperback)

ABOUT THE AUTHOR

Bridget Heos is the author of more than 60 children's books, including many advice and how-to titles. She lives safely in Kansas City with her husband and four children. You can find out more about her at www.authorbridgetheos.com.

ABOUT THE ILLUSTRATOR

Silvia Baroncelli has loved to draw since she was a child. She collaborates regularly with publishers in drawing and graphic design from her home in Prato, Italy. Her best collaborators are her four nephews, daughter Ginevra, and organized husband Tommaso. Find out more about her on the web at silviabaroncelli.it

It's hot, super heroes. And you've worked up a sweat saving a ton of people. You could cool off in the swimming pool. But let's go over some water safety rules before you dive in.

First, is a lifeguard on duty? Good.
Next you need a swimming buddy. If
you are in trouble, he can tell the lifeguard.

Super Dave has passed Level 1 swim class.

Later that summer. . .
Good job! You passed your swim test.
Time to get in.

Hold on. You can only dive in the diving area, where it's deep enough. Otherwise, you could hit your head on the bottom. Better jump feet first.

There's no running. You could slip. The lifeguard is whistling at you.

Cannonball!

You could swim. . .

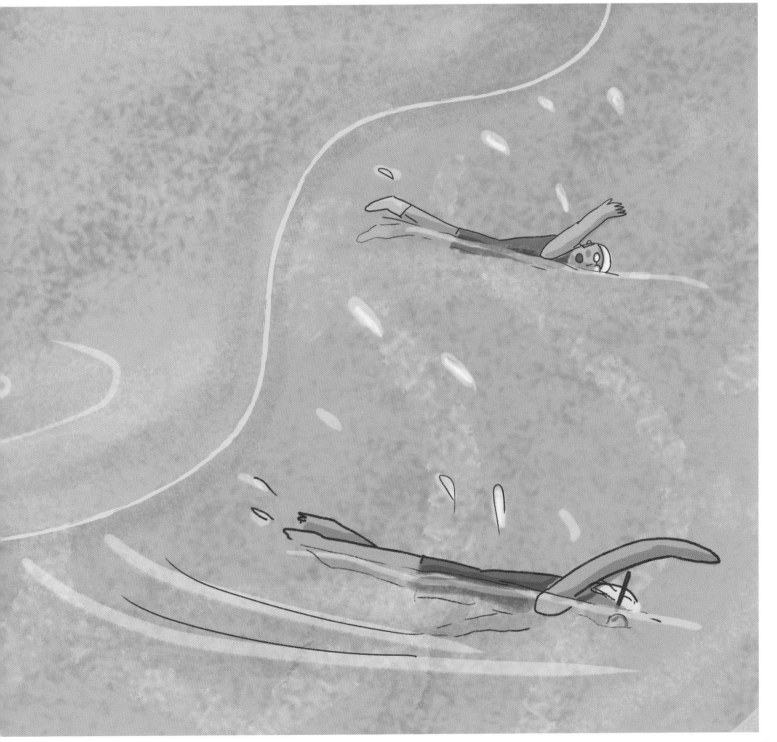

Boat safety is a little different. Everybody needs a life jacket. Stay seated while the boat is moving.

Last stop: the beach. Be careful when you step off the boat.

The ocean has waves, currents, and animals.
Flags show when it is unsafe to enter the water.

In the ocean, waves can make you tired.
Be sure to take breaks on the beach.

Battling an evil robotic jellyfish isn't much of a break.
Lounging is more like it. Just don't forget the sunscreen!

Here's one more tip: Swimming against a strong rip current will wear you out. . . even you, Aquatic Guy. Instead, swim parallel to shore until you are out of the current. Then swim in a diagonal line toward shore.

Uh-oh! A storm! Never swim when there is lightning. You could be electrocuted.

Ah, safe and dry. Swimming is fun, just be sure to do it safely.

SWIMMING SAFETY RULES TO REMEMBER

- Learn how to swim.
- Only swim when a lifeguard is on duty.
- An adult should also be with you.
- Have a swimming buddy.
- Follow pool safety rules, such as no running, roughhousing, or diving in shallow areas.
- On boats, wear a life jacket. Stay seated.
- At the beach, follow flag safety. Know how to swim safely through waves and currents.

GLOSSARY WORDS

electrocuted To be injured or killed by an electric shock.

life jacket A floatation device worn like a vest.

parallel A line alongside another line.

rip current A current that moves away from the shore. A current is like a river of water flowing in the ocean.

roughhousing Play fighting, such as wrestling.

wave A swell of water that breaks on the shore.

READ MORE

Kesselring, Susan. Being Safe Around Water. Mankato, Minn.: Child's World, 2011.

Knowlton, MaryLee. Safety Around Water. Stay Safe. New York: Crabtree, 2009.

Mara, Wil. What Should I Do? At the Pool. Community Connections. Ann Arbor, Mich.: Cherry Lake, 2012.

Rau, Dana Meachen. Water Safety. Bookworms: Safe Kids. New York: Benchmark Books, 2010.

WEBSITES

BEACH KIDS | U.S. EPA
http://water.epa.gov/learn/kids/ beachkids/index.cfm
Learn more about the beach and beach safety.

BOATING SAFETY SIDEKICKS
http://www.boatingsidekicks.com/besafe.htm
Learn more about boating safety from the National Safe Boating Council.

KIDS HEALTH: SWIMMING
http://kidshealth.org/kid/watch/out/ swim.html
Learn more about swimming safety in pools, lakes, ponds, water parks, and the ocean.

Every effort has been made to ensure that these websites are appropriate for children. However, because of the nature of the Internet, it is impossible to guarantee that these sites will remain active indefinitely or that their contents will not be altered.